Invasive Species Takeover

ZEBRA MUSSELS

SCOTT PEARSON

BLACK
RABBIT
BOOKS

Bolt is published by Black Rabbit Books
P.O. Box 3263, Mankato, Minnesota, 56002.
www.blackrabbitbooks.com
Copyright © 2017 Black Rabbit Books

Design and Production by Michael Sellner
Photo Research by Rhonda Milbrett

Library of Congress Control Number: 2015954919

HC ISBN: 978-1-68072-019-8   PB ISBN: 978-1-68072-283-3

Printed in the United States at CG Book Printers,
North Mankato, Minnesota, 56003. PO #1793 4/16

Web addresses included in this book were working and appropriate at the time of publication. The publisher is not responsible for broken or changed links.

Image Credits
Alamy: blickwinkel, 3, 20; blickwinkel/Hecker, 10; Dreams-time: Andrew Sabai, 24; Viter8, 31; Flickr: TownePost Network, 19; Getty: Peter Yates, 4–5; Newscom: Mark Hoffman/MCT, 32; Ron Offermans/Buiten–beeld/Minden Pictures, 28 (bottom); Public Domain: U.S. Fish & Wildlife Service, 14; Science Source: Ted Kinsman, 6; Scubaluna Photography: Flickr, Scubaluna Photography, Cover; Shutterstock: 1082492116, 28 (top); A_Lesik, 23 (bottom); Alex Kolokythas Photography, 13 (top); Anne Kitzman, 23 (top); sakhorn, 22; scubaluna, 27, 28 (middle); Vitalii Hulai, Back Cover, 1, 24–25, 8–9, 29
Every effort has been made to contact copyright holders for material reproduced in this book. Any omissions will be rectified in subsequent printings if notice is given to the publisher.

Contents

CHAPTER 1

Covered by

Shells

Monroe, Michigan, had a problem. There was no running water. Without water, the power plant had to shut down. The people looked for answers. Soon, they found the main water pipe was clogged. It was full of shells.

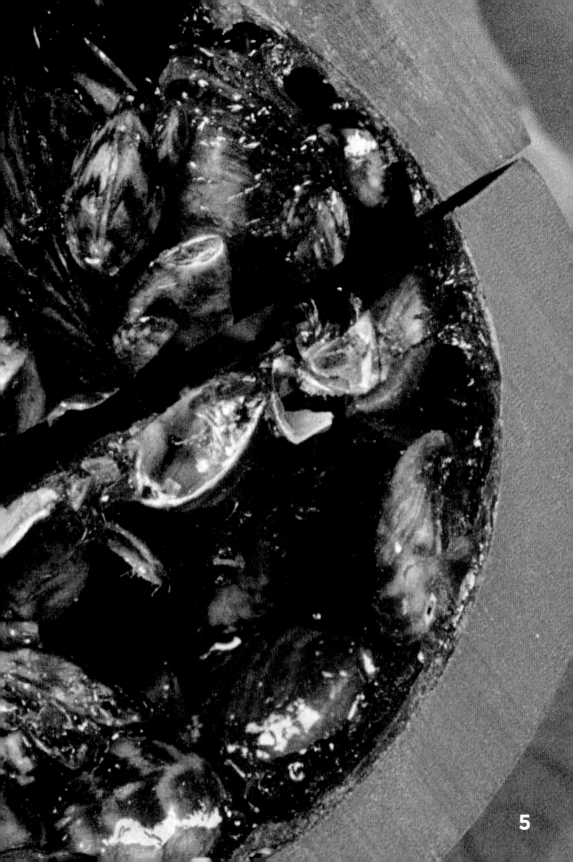

5

Sticking to Everything

The shells belonged to zebra mussels. Zebra mussels are animals that live underwater. And they stick to anything. They make their homes on rocks or in pipes.

Zebra mussels also stick together. Thousands of mussels clump together in an area. These large groups easily clog pipes.

Some mussels even live on other animals.

SIPHONS

SHELL

BYSSUS
(under body)

9

Invasive Species

The mussels in Monroe came from Lake Erie. But zebra mussels weren't supposed to be there. Several years ago, boats brought the mussels into U.S. lakes. These mussels spread to new areas. They hurt animals that already lived there. Zebra mussels are an **invasive species**.

CHAPTER 2

Mussels on the

Zebra mussels are from the Caspian and Black seas in **Eurasia**. Ships sailed in these seas. Then, the ships traveled across the ocean. The mussels came along. The first zebra mussels were discovered in the United States in 1988.

Great Lakes

Caspian Sea
Black Sea

Mussels Traveling the World

Spreading Fast

Birds and fish ate zebra mussels in Eurasia. They kept the mussel population low. But those **predators** weren't in North America. The mussels spread quickly. They hitched rides on boats. Then, they traveled to other lakes and rivers.

Zebra Mussels in U.S. Lakes

Today, zebra mussels live in about 700 out of **123,444** U.S. lakes.

Canada

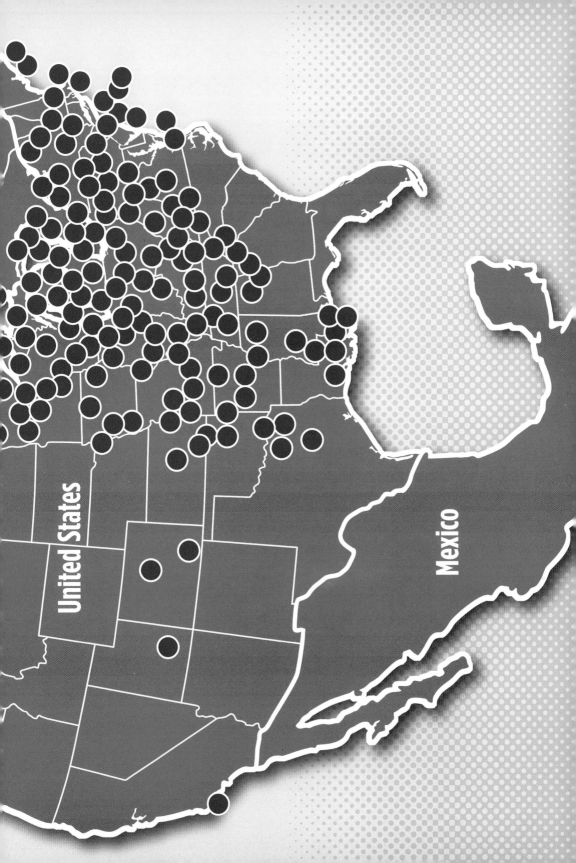

CHAPTER 3

Shells of Destruction

Zebra mussels cause a lot of trouble. They get inside boat engines. Then, they clog them up. **Props** can get so covered with mussels they can't turn.

The mussels' shells are very sharp. They can easily cut a swimmer's foot.

Killed by Mussels

Zebra mussels also hurt other water animals. They will live right on top of other mussels. The mussels underneath can't open their shells. They starve to death.

Zebra mussels eat tiny plants in the water. This eating cleans the water. But it also takes food away from other animals.

CHAPTER 4

Stopping Zebra Mussels

Zebra mussels usually get from place to place by sticking to boats. When a boat leaves the water, they stay on. When the boat is put into another lake, the mussels slide off.

To stop these riders, some states have passed laws. Boaters must check for mussels as they leave the water.

Cleaning Up after Boating

Search the boat for mussels.

Wash the boat with hot water.

Throw bait away.

Getting Rid of Mussels

Some **chemicals** kill zebra mussels. But these chemicals also kill other animals. Scientists are trying to find a safe way to get rid of the mussels.

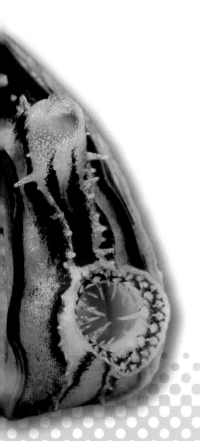

Zebra mussels can live out of water for more than a week.

Looking Forward

Zebra mussels are troublemakers. But they do a little good. They do help clean lake and river water. But without care, these creatures take over. That's why these invaders must be stopped.

ZEBRA MUSSELS BY THE NUMBERS

1 million

NUMBER OF EGGS A FEMALE LAYS IN A YEAR

2 years

AVERAGE LIFE SPAN

$5 BILLION

ESTIMATED AMOUNT SPENT TO STOP ZEBRA MUSSELS

10,000

NUMBER OF ZEBRA MUSSELS THAT CAN ATTACH TO ANOTHER MUSSEL

Think about It. . .

1. Chemicals kill zebra mussels. But many people don't want to use them. Use other sources to find out why chemicals might not be a good solution.

2. Boats carrying zebra mussels spread the creatures. How would you tell boaters about this problem?

3. What do you think should be done about zebra mussels? Use facts to support your answer.

GLOSSARY

byssus (BY-sus)—a strong, sticky thread that mussels use to attach themselves to surfaces

chemical (KE-muh-kuhl)—a substance that can cause a change in another substance

Eurasia (yur-AY-zhuh)—the two continents of Europe and Asia

invasive species (in-VAY-siv SPEE-seez)—animals or plants that spread through an area where they are not native, often causing problems for native plants and animals

predator (PRED-uh-tuhr)—an animal that eats other animals

prop (PRAHP)—a device with two or more blades that turns quickly to make a ship or aircraft move; prop is short for propeller.

siphon (SI-fun)—an organ used by mussels to suck in and then squirt out water

LEARN MORE

Kallio, Jamie. *12 Things to Know about Invasive Species.*
Today's News. Mankato, MN: Peterson Pub. Co., 2015.

O'Connor, Karen. *The Threat of Invasive Species.*
Animal 911: Environmental Threats. New York: Gareth
Stevens Publishing, 2014.

Spilsbury, Richard. *Invasive Species Underwater.*
Invaders from Earth. New York: PowerKids Press, 2015.

WEBSITES

Alien Profile: Zebra Mussel
**dnr.wi.gov/org/caer/ce/eek/critter/invert/
zebramussel.htm**

Frequently Asked Questions about the Zebra Mussel
**fl.biology.usgs.gov/Nonindigenous_Species/
Zebra_mussel_FAQs/zebra_mussel_faqs.html**

Zebra Mussel
**www.dnr.state.mn.us/invasives/aquaticanimals/
zebramussel/index.html**

INDEX

There is so much to explore in Australia!

LOOKING AROUND

Uluru is a huge **orange** rock in the desert.

Uluru is sacred to some of the first people of Australia. They believe their ancestors created the rock long ago.

COLORFUL ANIMALS

Find a rainbow of colors under the sea!

See **yellow** fish swim at the Great Barrier Reef.

The Reef is home to bright sea life such as **pink** coral.

Gray koalas nibble on tasty **green** leaves.

Rainbow lorikeets perch high in the trees.

Their **red** bills and **blue** heads are a bright sight.

Kangaroos take a break from hopping.

In **brown** grass, they search for food.

CELEBRATIONS AND FOOD

Red, yellow, and lime green shine in the night!

The Vivid Sydney festival celebrates art with colorful lights.

Pink and yellow fireworks fill the night sky.

Bright lights kick off a colorful New Year!

Time for a snack! Lamingtons are the perfect treat.

Brown chocolate and **white** coconut flakes cover soft cake.

Color is all around Australia!

MORE ABOUT AUSTRALIA!

Continent: Australia
Capital city: Canberra
Population: 23,470,145 (2018 estimate)

ARCTIC OCEAN

NORTH AMERICA

EUROPE

ASIA

ATLANTIC OCEAN

AFRICA

PACIFIC OCEAN

PACIFIC OCEAN

SOUTH AMERICA

INDIAN OCEAN

Australia

Canberra

SOUTHERN OCEAN

MANY COLORS

Australia has so many colors. Here are some of the Crayola colors used in this book.

BURNT SIENNA

SEA GREEN

PEACH

LASER LEMON

CERISE

GLOSSARY

ancestor: a real or mythical person who was in someone's family in past times

Australia: a continent in the South Pacific Ocean

celebrate: to do something special for an important event or holiday

continent: one of Earth's seven large landmasses

festival: a time of celebration in honor of a special occasion

firework: a bright light display that is loud and colorful when burned. Fireworks are often used at celebrations.

Great Barrier Reef: a large system of coral reefs off Australia's northeastern coast. The Great Barrier Reef is the biggest coral reef system in the world.

sacred: holy or deserving great respect

TO LEARN MORE

Books

Dean, Jessica. *Australia: All around the World*. Minneapolis: Jump!, 2019.

Leigh, Anna. *Meet a Baby Kangaroo*. Minneapolis: Lerner Publications, 2018.

Parkes, Elle. *Let's Explore Australia*. Minneapolis: Lerner Publications, 2018.

Websites

Crayola: Coral Reef and Seaweed
https://www.crayola.com/crafts/coral-reef-and-seaweed-craft/

National Geographic Kids: Australia
https://kids.nationalgeographic.com/explore/countries/australia/

INDEX

PHOTO ACKNOWLEDGMENTS

Image credits: Juergen Freund/Alamy Stock Photo, p. 1; Olga Kashubin/Shutterstock.com, p. 4 (opera house); Auscape/Universal Images Group/Getty Images, pp. 4 (flowering plant), 8; Jordi Prat Puig/Shutterstock.com, p. 4 (beach boxes); Dwi Yulianto/EyeEm/Getty Images, p. 5 (lizard); Thurtell/E+/Getty Images, p. 5 (girl); davidf/iStock/ Getty Images, pp. 6–7; Doug Perrine/Nature Picture Library/Alamy Stock Photo, p. 9; Adam J/Shutterstock.com, p. 10; Konrad Wothe/Minden Pictures/Getty Images, p. 11; oxime/iStock/Getty Images, p. 12; Zhong Zhenbin/Anadolu Agency/Getty Images, p. 14; James D. Morgan/Getty Images, p. 15; Scott Barbour/City of Sydney/Getty Images, p. 17; Belinda Howell/Moment/Getty Images, p. 18; Laura Westlund/Independent Picture Service, p. 20 (map); Ramberg/iStock/Getty Images, p. 20 (flag).

Cover: jspix/imageBROKER/Getty Images (koala bear); Piter Lenk/Alamy Stock Photo (beach huts); Nigel Marsh/ iStock/Getty Images (coral reef); Konrad Wothe/Minden Pictures/Getty Images (birds).